Fairy Magic

Also by Rosemary Ellen Guiley

Ask the Angels
An Angel in Your Pocket
A Miracle in Your Pocket

Fairy Magic

All about fairies and how to bring their magic into your life

☆

Rosemary Ellen Guiley

Element
An Imprint of HarperCollins*Publishers*
77–85 Fulham Palace Road
Hammersmith, London W6 8JB

The website address is:
www.thorsonselement.com

and *Element* are trademarks of
HarperCollins*Publishers* Limited

First published by Element 2004

3 5 7 9 10 8 6 4 2

© Rosemary Ellen Guiley 2004

Rosemary Ellen Guiley asserts the moral right to
be identified as the author of this work

A catalogue record of this book
is available from the British Library

ISBN 0 00 715129 2

Printed and bound in Great Britain by
Martins the Printers Ltd, Berwick upon Tweed

Contents

Introduction

I once lived in a house in a wooded area in New England, and it was there that I had my introduction to the fairy realm. I felt as though I'd acquired my own private nature preserve. I could sit on the back deck and look out over a brook populated with muskrats and ducks and trees filled with an abundance of birds. Soon I discovered that another, largely unseen population existed in the landscape: nature spirits. I became aware of the spirits especially at times when I was in a peaceful mood, not thinking of anything in particular, but simply drinking in the beauty, scents and sounds of the environment around me. Mostly I noticed them at dusk when long shadows fell across the woods, and also at dawn when shapes emerged from the lightening darkness. Nights when pale moonlight glittered through the trees were magical; the woods came alive with mysterious presences.

I rarely 'saw' the beings, but rather sensed them with my inner eye. There were silvery-white forms that zipped and flitted about the woods; strange little creatures that seemed to be made of bark and leaves; and other beings that I would simply call 'presences'. These latter ones seemed more like essences of the natural world than creatures or beings.

Whatever I perceived, I usually could only hold them in my consciousness for a few moments at a time. Later I learned how to expand my 'fairy sight' to have more detailed perception, both inner and visual, and I also learned how to establish relationships with some of these beings. In this book I will share with you how I did that, and also describe the rewards that come with a sincere partnership with the nature kingdom.

My awareness of the nature spirits was part of my unfolding awareness of the angelic kingdom. I discovered I wasn't alone in this, by any means, but that many people were having similar spiritual awakenings and encounters with angels and fairies. What does it all mean?

Humanity has sent out a collective call to the spiritual realms for assistance. We have received a calling in return. If we wish the spiritual help of angels and fairies in our own personal growth and in our striving to make the world a better and more harmonious place, then we must establish relationships that reach beyond the bounds of physical earth. We must demonstrate our sincere intent to make use of the help that is offered. Fairies and angels were created as helping beings, to look after all things in accordance to the Divine Plan. They all work toward a purpose of wholeness and love.

Angels have the primary responsibility of looking after the wellbeing of people, while nature spirits, tending to the natural realm, traditionally have had different interactions with us. But now the nature spirits have made themselves available to open more lines of communication with humans. An earth of beauty, harmony and love cannot be accomplished by one force alone. The fairies cannot do it alone, the angels cannot do it alone, and we humans cannot do it alone. It requires cooperation. Fairies, like angels, can help us bring forth joy and abundance into the world.

The fairy universe teems with diverse beings. This book is an introduction to their marvellous and magical world, and how you can participate in it. As you turn the pages, imagine that you are showered with glittery fairy dust that casts a special enchantment to transport you through the Golden Door. And what is the Golden Door, and what lies beyond it? That's for you to discover!

ROSEMARY ELLEN GUILEY, PH.D.

1
Into the Fairy Realm

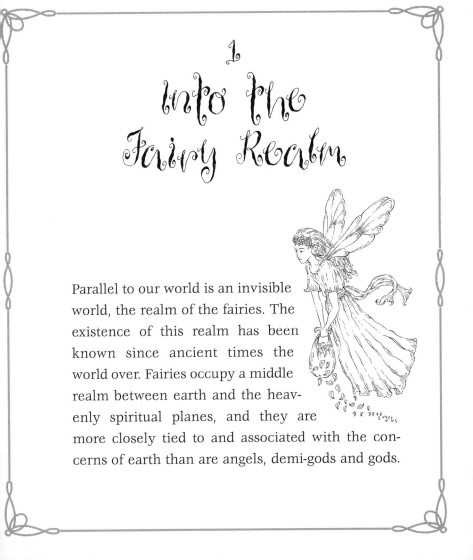

Parallel to our world is an invisible world, the realm of the fairies. The existence of this realm has been known since ancient times the world over. Fairies occupy a middle realm between earth and the heavenly spiritual planes, and they are more closely tied to and associated with the concerns of earth than are angels, demi-gods and gods.

Descriptions of fairies and explanations of their origins vary, as do the nature of human interactions with fairies. Some fairies are feared and others are courted. They are supernaturally endowed and can do magic, and for that reason people throughout the ages have sought their help and favours.

Perhaps you've already glimpsed their secret world as they work industriously in nature and around human households and places of work. Fairies are elusive, and many prefer to keep to themselves. However, it is possible to build a relationship with the fairy realm that is rewarding and productive. This book will tell you how to do it.

Fairies are supernaturally

endowed and can do magic,

and for that reason people

throughout the ages have sought

their help and favours.

Origins of fairies

The term 'fairy' comes from the Latin word *fata*, or fate, which refers to the Fates of mythology: three women who spin, twist and cut the threads of life. 'Fairy' came into usage in medieval times and was often used to refer to women who had magical powers. 'Fairy' originally meant 'fae-erie', or a state of enchantment. According to lore, fairies themselves do not like the word, but prefer such labels as 'the Good Neighbours', 'the Gentry', 'the People of Peace', 'the Strangers', 'Themselves', 'The Seely (Blessed) Court' and similar terms. Fairies are often referred to as 'the Little People'.

Fairy beliefs are universal and, despite their variations, are strikingly similar. While their lore can be found around the world, fairy beliefs are particularly strong in the British Isles and in Europe.

Contemporary popular Western beliefs about angels link fairies to angels as a subordinate class of beings, in accordance with the idea of ministering angels – everything in nature has its guiding, or ministering, angel. In folklore tradition, however, fairies are not a type of heavenly angel, but a separate class of being.

Fairy lore is older than Christianity, but much of it has acquired Christian elements. The major explanations for the origins of fairies are:

✦ They are the souls of the pagan dead. Those who were not baptized Christian became at death trapped between heaven and earth.

✦ They are the guardians of the dead. Their realm is a between-place between the realm of the living and the realm of the dead.

✦ They are themselves the ghosts of venerated ancestors.

✦ They are fallen angels who were cast out of heaven with Lucifer but condemned by God to remain in the elements of the earth.

✦ They are nature spirits who are attached to particular places or to the four elements.

✦ They are supernatural creatures who are monsters or half-human, half-monster.

✦ They are small-statured human beings, a primitive race that went into hiding in order to survive.

In all likelihood, there is no one origin or explanation of fairies. Some may be nature spirits and elementals, others belong to the realm of supernatural forces, others are associated with the land of the dead, and still others have a distant relationship to humans.

Types and descriptions of fairies

Fairies have many names and descriptions. They usually are invisible save to those with clairvoyant sight. They can make themselves visible to humans if they so desire. Some are diminutive, even tiny, while others are huge, larger than humans. Some are beautiful and some are ugly. Some resemble humans, while others are spirit-like, with wings.

Some are morally ambivalent, while others are always benevolent, and still others are believed to be always malevolent, such as those that guard certain places in nature, or who like to trick the unwary traveller.

Some fairies are solitary, especially those that inhabit the wild. Others live as a fairy race or nation, usually said to be underground and accessed through mounds, caves, burrows and holes in the ground. The Land of Fairy, also called Elfland, has characteristics of the land of the dead. Time is altered, so that a day in human life might stretch into years in fairyland. There is no day or night, but a perpetual twilight.

Modern concepts of fairies divide them into four main groups aligned with the four elements of nature:

✦ **Earth fairies** are associated with gardens, woodlands, nature, flora, animals, minerals, places in nature, mines, caves, and so on. Earth fairies also include those who work in human households, such as brownies. Dwarfs, gnomes, elves, pixies, trolls and knockers are earth-oriented fairies.

✦ **Water fairies** inhabit lakes, rivers, ponds and other bodies of water, including seas and oceans. Sprites, nymphs, selkies and mermaids are among the many kinds of water fairies.

✦ **Air fairies**, often called sylphs, govern the winds, clouds and weather. They are especially associated with storms and tempests.

✦ **Fire fairies** live in wild fires, volcanoes, bonfires, the fires of the home hearth and electricity.

Activities of fairies

Fairies take care of and guard the world of nature. The interactions of fairies with humans depend upon the kind of fairy and its purpose. For example, a fairy of a river will not have as much interaction with humans as a fairy who looks after human tools.

Traditionally, the existence and activities of fairies have explained the reasons for illnesses, deformities and untimely deaths among children; epidemics among livestock, and various disasters of weather. Fairies bewitched animals and people. They stole human women for wives. And, they stole human babies and substituted their own sickly children, or changelings, in their place.

In order to stay in the good graces of fairies, humans kept clean houses and left out food and drink. In return, fairies bestowed gifts, luck, fertility and money, and helped humans with their chores. Fairies also were given offerings at sacred wells, fountains, lakes, tree groves and other places said to be 'fairy haunts', so that humans could ward off illness and misfortune.

The folk concept of benign or malignant fairies is often ambiguous. Whatever the disposition of a particular fairy or group of fairies, human respect for them is essential. Many folk tales illustrate the desirability of kindness, politeness, observance of taboos and correct etiquette in dealing with the fairies.

Human respect for fairies

is essential.

Why work with fairies?

Many people are still careful of the fairy folk, but today our relationship with them has changed in more beneficial and productive ways. We have advanced in our understanding of our relationships with the unseen and spiritual realms, and we are more desirous of establishing a cooperative partnership with them.

We have much we can learn from the fairy realm. Their roles in nature and the living forces of nature, their ability to move about time and space, and their seemingly magical ability to manifest things are not limited to only them. In lore, fairies bestow their magical gifts as favours. By cultivating cooperative relationships with them, we stand to learn how to bring their magic into our world.

Working with fairies also makes us more aware of our impact on the natural world and increases our respect for all things in nature. We cannot abuse the natural world through waste, destruction and pollution and expect it to sustain us. Creation is a balance of giving and receiving. We must support the natural world in order to be supported by it.

The fairy realm knows only too keenly the negative effects of human ignorance. It is in their interests to engage us in communication and mutual work, and they respond whenever we send out a sincere intent.

By cultivating cooperative

relationships with fairies, we stand

to learn how to bring their

magic into our world.

What is fairy magic?

Fairy magic is the establishment of communication and a working partnership with the fairy realm. It is magical in that it takes us beyond our limited physical world into other states of awareness that advance our personal and spiritual growth.

Fairy magic is simple. It is not a magic laden with odd procedures or rituals, but is an expansion of consciousness that anyone can attain.

In 1691, Reverend Robert Kirk of Scotland wrote a now-famous essay on fairies, *The Secret Commonwealth (of Elves, Fauns and Fairies)*, which was published in 1815. Kirk described the Scottish fairy lore of his times, and gave two techniques for developing fairy sight, or the clairvoyant ability to perceive fairies:

1. Take a tether of hair which has bound a corpse to a bier. Wind it around your waist. Stoop down and look backwards through your legs until a funeral procession passes.

2. Find an accomplished seer. Have him (or her) place his right foot over your left foot and lay his hand on your head. This will confer clairvoyant power to you.

One can only wonder if readers actually obtained fairy sight in either of these manners!

Acquiring fairy sight is far less complicated. Follow the simple tips in this book to open a truly magical and wonderful world.

Fairy magic is not a magic laden

with odd procedures or rituals, but is

an expansion of consciousness that

anyone can attain.

2
Devas, Fairies and Angels

Perhaps you have heard the term 'deva' applied to fairies, nature spirits or angels. What exactly are devas, and what is their proper place in relationship to fairies and angels?

The term 'deva' is Sanskrit, and means 'shining one'. In Eastern spirituality, there are different types of devas. For example, Hinduism recognizes three. The first is a brahman in the form of a personal God. A brahman is an abstract concept expressing absolute being or absolute consciousness, a state of pure transcendence that defies precise description. The second is a mortal who has attained a state of divinity, but remains mortal. The third is an enlightened person who has realized God.

In Buddhism, a deva is a god who lives in one of the 28 good celestial realms. Formerly mortal, they enjoy a long and happy life in these realms as rewards for their good earthly lives. However, they are subject to the wheel of reincarnation and still must overcome attachments that require them to reincarnate.

In popular Western spirituality, a deva is an advanced spirit or god-being who governs the elementals and nature spirits and the wellbeing of all things in nature. Thus, the devas can be seen as a type of administrator or manager. They are of a more refined energy than the fairy realm, closer to that of angels. When perceived clairvoyantly, they have flowing, shining forms of various colours.

Are devas angel or fairy? Actually, it is impossible to completely separate the spiritual realms, for they flow into each other. Devas more or less occupy a middle realm between fairies and angels.

In popular Western spirituality,

a deva is an advanced spirit or

god-being who governs the

elementals and nature spirits and the

wellbeing of all things in nature.

Devas in nature

Our ideas about devas have developed out of Theosophy, a spiritual philosophy based on Eastern concepts that was introduced to the West largely through the writings of Helena P. Blavatsky in the late nineteenth century. Blavatsky was a co-founder of the Theosophical Society in New York City. She said she received much of her information from communication with various ascended masters who served as her mentors.

According to Blavatsky, devas are types of angels or gods who cannot be worshipped by humans. They are progressed entities from a previous planetary period. After our solar system formed, they arrived on earth before either elementals or man, and remained dormant until a certain stage of human evolution was reached. When our spiritual consciousness was mature enough to recognize and work with them, the devas became an active force and integrated with the elementals to further the development of humanity.

Blavatsky said that devas are under the ministry of the archangels. The vast army of solar and planetary angels are called the Army of the Light or the Hosts of the Logos. Each planet, each solar system, each type of being has an archangelic regent, supported by legions of lesser devas. She envisioned orders of devas intertwined with gods and angels, all responsible for every minute creation in the universe. Mountain Gods preside over the peaks, while Landscape Angels rule over the divisions and areas of the earth's surface. Builder Angels use the Archetypes to create the lesser spirits, humans, animals, plants and rocks. Guardian Angels watch over humans, their homes, children and endeavours, while Healing Angels tend the sick, heal the wounded and console the bereaved. Ruler Angels guide and direct nations in the fulfilment of their destiny. Devas of Nature provide the spark of life to the Builders' creations and nurture each being's existence. Within this category are the nature spirits who tend the earth, air, fire and water – the brownies, sylphs, salamanders and undines – as well as the gods of storms, fire and weather. Devas of Art and Beauty lift up the beautiful in all things, while the Angels of Music bear the Voice of God, in all its complicated melodies, to mankind.

Thus through Theosophy, devas came to be regarded as high-level nature spirits. Even though they are involved in the spiritual growth of humans, they pursue their own work and are more distant to us than much of the fairy realm. When contacted psychically, they often deliver messages in which they express their dismay with our pollution of the earth and disrespect for nature. However, their unhappiness is tempered with love and willingness to help us get our spiritual act together – if we will follow through with positive action as a result of our contact with them.

Like many residents of the fairy realm, devas will gladly work with individuals who have the proper respect and attunement. Their work involves creating higher frequencies of spiritual energies, especially for healing. For example, they are actively involved in creating and producing homeopathic flower essences and healing gardens. Gardeners who work with devas consider them to be 'architects' of nature; one is assigned to every living thing, even the soil. Devas design blueprints for all living things, and orchestrate the energies necessary for growth and health. Devas dispense advice on planting, fertilizing, watering and general plant care, as well as how to eliminate pests such as moles and worms without killing them. The relationship with devas goes much deeper, to include a heightened respect for all living things and for nature, to work with unseen realms in love and cooperation, and to realize the interconnectedness of all things and to God.

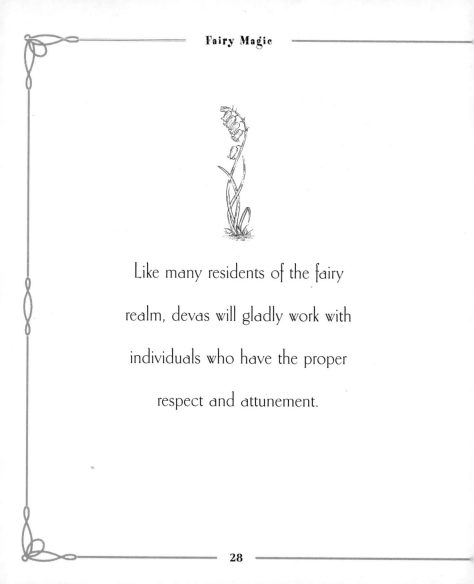

Like many residents of the fairy

realm, devas will gladly work with

individuals who have the proper

respect and attunement.

Miracles at Findhorn

A breakthrough in our awareness of the devic world developed at Findhorn, a spiritual community in northern Scotland that became renowned in the 1960s and 1970s for spectacular produce grown with the advice of devas.

The founders of Findhorn were Peter and Eileen Caddy, husband and wife, and their friend, Dorothy Maclean. In 1962, the three found themselves out of work in Scotland – they had for years worked together running resort hotels – and they took up residence at the Findhorn Bay Caravan Travel Park, where the Caddys had their trailer. The area was desolate, but Peter Caddy felt he had been directed there for a purpose through spiritual guidance that Eileen had received in meditation.

The Caddys and Maclean had devoted themselves to spiritual study for years. Peter had a keen sense of intuition. Eileen had mediumistic gifts. Maclean channelled divinely inspired messages.

Peter gardened to pass the time, even though the sandy soil and the inhospitable climate were not auspicious. In May 1963, their world changed forever. Maclean received an unusual message about the 'forces of Nature', and that one of her jobs was to attune and harmonize with those forces, who would be friendly in their greeting to her. Peter interpreted it to mean that she could get guidance from Nature on what to do in the garden. This was immediately affirmed in her next meditation, with a message that cooperation not only would be possible, but would be welcomed with great joy. The communicating being told Maclean that she could attune to nature spirits and the higher nature spirits over them, that is, the spirits of the clouds, rain and vegetables. The being told her, 'Just be open and seek into the glorious realms of Nature with sympathy and understanding, knowing that these beings are of the Light, willing to help but suspicious of humans and on the lookout for the false. Keep with me and they will not find it, and you will all build towards the new.'

Maclean did as instructed. The first nature spirit to come into her awareness was the 'Pea Deva', which she described as holding the archetypal pattern in place for all the peas in the world. Her primary contact emerged as the 'Landscape Angel', who had a broad, holistic outlook. The Landscape Angel often facilitated communication between Maclean and other beings. All communications were on the inner planes.

Initially, Maclean did not know what to call the beings with whom she came in contact. She thought them to be angels, but the term 'angel' conjured up to her hackneyed pop culture images. These beings seemed too glorious. She settled on the term 'deva', though in talking about them, she used the terms 'angel', 'deva' and 'nature spirit' interchangeably. (Later, years after leaving Findhorn, Maclean reverted to 'angel'.) She never saw these beings with external vision, but sensed them on the inner planes. They were of awesome scope, she said. Their duties were to hold the archetypal pattern of all material things in place – even manmade objects such as machines – and to offer love to humankind. Within a year, under the guidance of the devas, Findhorn had been transformed. Cabbages, normally four pounds at maturity, weighed over forty pounds. Broccoli grew so large they were too heavy to lift from the ground.

In 1966, a friend of Peter Caddy's, scholar R. Ogilvie Crombie, visited Findhorn. Evidently, he appealed to the nature spirits, for after his return home to Edinburgh, a nature spirit appeared to him one day in the Royal Botanic Gardens. It was about three feet high and was half man and half animal. It introduced itself to Crombie as Kurmos, and said he lived in the gardens and helped trees to grow. Kurmos soon introduced Crombie to Pan, the chief of the nature spirits. Pan told Crombie that he had been chosen to help renew the lost contact between mankind and the nature spirits. Crombie relayed Pan's messages to Findhorn.

Findhorn attracted people from all over the world who wanted to participate in building an exciting new 'community of light' that was ushering in a new era of cooperation between man and the kingdom of nature.

Brian Nobbs, a British professional potter and artist, arrived at Findhorn in 1970, to find the place filled with magic and light. Nobbs, who ran the pottery, became Crombie's heir apparent with the community of Pan. It proved to be a purposeful passing of the spiritual wand, for Crombie died in 1974, and Nobbs became instrumental in the preservation of the devic presence at Findhorn.

In the summer of 1971, Nobbs travelled to Edinburgh, and was invited by Crombie to spend the weekend with him. Crombie suggested that they spend a day visiting various places of devic importance, including the Royal Botanic Gardens. Crombie instructed Nobbs to be as aware as possible. 'When you notice something, tell me,' he said. 'But I won't give you any clues.'

The day was momentous, in which Nobbs experienced a tremendous expansion of consciousness that was, he said, 'mind-shattering'. One of the most potent sites was the Royal Botanic Gardens, where Crombie himself had first encountered Pan.

'It was as though the scales dropped away from my eyes and senses,' said Nobbs. 'Everything was magnified dozens of times. I found myself wading through waves of energy rippling around my ankles like electrical currents.' Crombie explained to him that these were energy lines connecting different points, like leys. Nobbs's attention then was directed off to one side of their path, where he sensed, with his inner vision, a being standing and regarding them. It was Pan. 'Yes,' agreed Crombie, when Nobbs told him of his impression. 'Pan has been wondering how long it would take you to notice him.'

At the Hermitage, Nobbs walked about feeling a beam of light that entered him through the top of his head. He became aware of beautiful, human-like beings about four feet in height who accompanied them. 'I wasn't seeing this with my physical eyes,' he said. 'I thought I was mad.' But the impressions were real. Crombie called the beings 'high elves' after J.R.R. Tolkien's popular *Lord of the Rings* fantasy novels. The beings seemed happy to be described that way.

Crombie then explained to Nobbs that the purpose of this encounter was for one of the beings to accompany him back to Findhorn, in order to make a link with the garden and the power points in it. 'And travel with me he did,' said Nobbs. 'I took the bus back to Findhorn, and he sat in the seat beside me. It was a very strange experience.'

In 1980, Peter and Eileen Caddy parted company; Peter went to America and Eileen remained at Findhorn. Nobbs went to America for several years, where he also encountered Pan.

In Pennsylvania, Nobbs lived in an area where there were few houses, and the garden abutted a forest. The nights were heavy with magic. 'One night I woke up to see the room flooded with a bright green light,' Nobbs said. 'I found I couldn't move – I was paralysed. Standing by the bed was an Indian in a loin cloth and a beaded necklace. He was green and his head touched the ceiling, which meant he was about nine feet in height.' The being simply regarded Nobbs – no message was transmitted. Nobbs was not frightened, despite his inability to move. After a short time, the figure faded away.

Nobbs was puzzled about the identity of the Indian. Several years later, he learned about the Indian deity, 'Living Solid Face' or 'The Mask Being', who ruled over the forests and wild things. It was another aspect of Pan.

Nobbs encountered this entity again in Florida near St Petersburg. He was walking along an urban street, thinking about Pan, and suddenly felt the weight of an invisible arm around his shoulder. It was his old friend, Pan. The two communed silently for about a hundred yards, and then Pan departed. The purpose of the encounter seemed to be to let Nobbs know that the beings of the nature kingdom are with us always, even in urban environments.

Today Findhorn describes itself as an 'international spiritual community' founded on the principles that 'God, or the source of life, is accessible to each of us at all times, and that nature, including the planet, has intelligence and is part of a much larger plan. While we have no formal doctrine or creed, we believe an evolutionary expansion of consciousness is taking place in the world, creating a human culture infused with spiritual values.' Findhorn is a charitable trust foundation, and offers various spiritual educational and training programs.

Peter died in an auto accident in Europe in 1994. Eileen remains at Findhorn as a spiritual anchor. Since leaving Findhorn, Maclean has lived in Canada and the United States.

The Findhorn influence in America

The Findhorn model has inspired many people all around the world to engage in an active relationship with the devic and fairy realms. In America, two examples are Perelandra and Green Hope Farm.

Perelandra, located near Jeffersonton, Virginia, was founded by Machaelle Small Wright and her partner, Clarence Wright. It was named after Perelandra, or Venus, the planet of perfection in the science fiction novel of the same name by C.S. Lewis. In 1974, Machaelle opened psychically, and two years later began communicating with 'overlighting intelligences in nature' – her term for what others might call devas or nature spirits – and following their guidance for creating and cultivating the gardens. Perelandra is open to visitors once a year.

Green Hope Farm, near Meriden, New Hampshire, was founded by Molly and Jim Sheehan. It is privately owned and is not open to visitors. Molly Sheehan, a long-time gardening enthusiast who grew up on a farm in Connecticut, experienced a psychic opening in 1984, and began a spiritual quest that led to communion with the devic and angelic kingdoms.

One day she felt a distinct shift in her consciousness, and began getting 'little messages' from the plants. The voices were of the angels, devas and elementals involved with the plants. They gave her gardening guidance. Most important was their advice for geometric designs of gardens that the beings said would amplify the energetic properties of the plants, especially for healing. Like the founders of Findhorn, the Sheehans followed the advice, and began producing flower essence remedies.

Molly prefers not to label the beings as 'devas' or 'angels' or 'nature spirits'. The labels, she says, are too limiting and do not do justice to the beings. She perceives them as 'a spectrum of energy' whose nuances can be detected by shifts in vibrations. She senses that devas possess a 'bigger' energy than do angels, and are more evolved. However, archangels such as Michael seem bigger than devas.

Initially, Sheehan spent hours in meditation in order to communicate with the intelligences. Over time and with lots of practice, she perfected her ability so that communication became easier, especially through automatic writing.

Sheehan says that the purpose of Green Hope Farm is to demonstrate how the angelic, elemental and human kingdoms can work harmoniously together and with God. The angelic kingdom holds the vision and divine plan for the place, and inspires the human kingdom with love and inspiration. The elementals bring the divine plan into physical form, using humans as their 'hands and feet'.

Appearances of devas

Many nature spirits and fairies have the ability to project human-like forms, but because devas are on different and more subtle energy frequencies, they rarely do so. Many devas are sensed and felt and are not seen, except clairvoyantly. Some manifest more like angels: as pillars and balls of light or flowing colours. You may have the impression that they cannot be defined by any shape, but simply exist as large – and even fathomless – fields of energy.

Many devas are sensed and felt and

are not seen, except clairvoyantly.

Keys to the kingdom

In these two chapters, we have described quite a range of beings, yet they are only a few of the numbers of fairy, nature and deva beings. As you can see, experiences of them are subjective, and making distinctions among them is often difficult. However, emerging from these experiences are three universal 'keys to the kingdom' of the nature gods:

1. Contact with the fairy/deva realms requires a respectful and sincere approach. If they detect deception and insincerity, they will avoid you.

2. In order to communicate, you must develop your ability to attune to their energy and vibration. Trust your intuition and impressions of shapes and names. Resist trying to force-fit your experiences into labels.

3. Take action to manifest something positive as a result of your relationship.

The next chapter features ways you can train yourself to develop 'fairy sight', or the attunement to perceive fairies and devas.

3

Developing
Fairy
Awareness

In childhood, our psychic sense is more open and receptive to the invisible realms. In most people, this sense narrows and even closes as we near adulthood and become more  focused on the material world. Sometimes disapproving adults in our life can discourage the use of psychic sense.

By adulthood, most of us think that only specially gifted individuals have the ability to perceive and communicate with beings like fairies, devas and angels. This is not so, for anyone can reopen the psychic sense. 'Imagination is the bridge,' says Molly Sheehan, the co-founder of Green Hope Farm. 'Things that we think are our imagination are really messages. The more attention I paid to the messages, the more I realized that we are always connected.'

Fairies usually are perceived by the inner eye. That is, we have a mental impression of them. 'Fairy sight' is the ability to have a clairvoyant impression of fairies. Actually, fairy sight involves all the senses – it is more of a total psychic awareness. In addition to mental visual impressions, we may have psychic tactile sensations, sounds, smells – and even tastes.

The exercises in this chapter will help you to develop your fairy awareness by training your consciousness to expand.

'Fairy sight' is the ability to have a

clairvoyant impression of fairies.

Harmony with nature

One of the best ways to develop fairy awareness is to experience a genuine harmony with the natural world. Spending time in nature cultivates an attunement to its rhythms, both in the visible world and in the invisible realm of spirit.

One summer I visited Findhorn and had my own experience of Pan. Because of its latitude, Findhorn is nearly a land of the midnight sun at the solstice, and hosts a traditional Celtic Midsummer Festival. It sounded magical, and so I arranged to stay on campus for several days and participate in the activities.

I was immediately enchanted with the magical feel of the place. A wild and primitive atmosphere still envelops the landscape, and those who seek contact with the nature spirits – and are pure of heart in their intent – are still rewarded, as they were years ago when Findhorn was but an idea in the spiritual realms.

I took frequent hikes to the beach, winding first through trees and then through thickets of gorse, a scrubby brush that grows in the sandy soil. I paid attention to all the elements and felt myself a part of them. I fell into complete harmony with the environment, as though we were extensions of one another. In the evenings when twilight took over, I could shift my consciousness and perceive the glow of nature spirits, shining like points of lights.

I knew that if the nature gods approved of you, Pan himself might make himself known. One day when I was hiking alone to the beach, I suddenly heard the distinct sound of panpipes, Pan's musical flute, behind me. Thinking first that someone from the village was coming up behind me, I turned, but the trail was empty. I had no human company. I resumed walking. The soft music, faint at times, accompanied me until I was out of the gorse and on to open sand.

The experiences of the fairy lights and Pan were products of the inner harmony I felt with my environment. Besides spending relaxed time in nature, we can cultivate harmony in other ways.

Mindfulness

The great artist Raphael is said to have once told Leonardo da Vinci, 'I have noticed that when one paints, one should think of nothing: everything then comes better.'

Raphael was expressing the value of mindfulness. When he painted, Raphael did not allow himself to become distracted with thoughts about anything other than what he was doing. In thinking 'of nothing', he was focusing his full attention upon his art, and all of his energy thus flowed directly onto the canvas.

Most of us live nearly our entire lives somewhere else besides the present. We rehash the past and anticipate the future. All we ever have, however, is *now*.

Mindfulness means devoting yourself to one thing at a time. It means being fully present in what you are doing. The practice of mindfulness develops extended consciousness and the mental focus for harmony. Here are two easy exercises:

NATURE MINDFULNESS

Choose a spot outdoors. It can be your backyard, a park or a more exotic locale.

Relax and centre yourself in a meditative frame of consciousness. You can accomplish this easily by using the breath in a simple, three-step method.

Three-step breath technique

Step 1: On the intake and exhalation of breath, relax. Release the tension from your body until you feel light and fluid.

Step 2: On the intake and exhalation of breath, centre yourself in the still point within. This helps to eliminate outer distractions.

Step 3: On the intake and exhalation of breath, expand your consciousness into the space around you. This gently opens your awareness to spiritual planes.

As you breathe, visualize golden-white light flowing down from heaven through the top of your head. It fills your body as running water fills a vessel. See it flowing out through the soles of your feet into the planet. In this way, you will be open to the heavens and firmly grounded to the earth. When you breathe out, feel the light expand within you.

You can go through the steps slowly, using as many intakes of breath as necessary for you to feel you have accomplished each step. The more you practise, the more quickly you will be able to attain meditative consciousness — even in three single breaths, one for each step.

Once you feel relaxed and centred, use the breath as a way of feeling yourself expand.

As you exhale, you are expanding into the environment around you. It's as though you have an extra set of eyes, ears, hands and so forth that reach far beyond you.

When you feel ready, select five objects at random.
Five is the number of change, especially spiritual
change. Thus it is the number of the intuition.

Start with objects near you, and then move out
to more distant ones. They might be flowers,
bushes, trees, stones, clouds, hills, or whatever
draws your attention. It might also be an
animal, such as a squirrel foraging for food.

Observe each in as much detail as possible,
as though you are seeing it for the first and
last time in your life.

Imagine a line of white and gold light extending
from your heart to the heart of each thing you
selected. Feel this connection. Now extend the
connection to all of nature.

Ask for a message from the fairy realm. Allow impressions to arise spontaneously within you.

What do you experience? Record your thoughts and impressions.

HOME MINDFULNESS

Do the same exercise indoors. Go around your home and select five objects at random from any room. Arrange the objects in a row in front of you. Gaze at them one by one and as a group.

One by one, pick up each object and give it your full attention. Observe colours, textures, imperfections, symmetry. Look at it as though you were seeing it for the first and last time in your life. Think about its origin and its purpose, who made it, its usefulness and its place in your home.

Try to see what is hidden, for example, the underside or back of an object. Let your extended senses function like a periscope. Validate your impressions.

Ask for messages from the household fairies. What do they have to say about the objects? About your relationship to the objects, and to your home?

Record your experience.

Expanded listening

With practice, we can attune our inner ear to hear beyond the physical realm. The following two exercises are easy to do on a regular basis.

LISTENING TO THE OUTER WORLD

In your own home, settle into a comfortable
spot and use the three-step breath technique
on page 56 to enter into a meditative state with
your eyes closed. Allow the silence to thicken
around you. Listen to the sounds of the
environment around you: cars passing by on
the street, aeroplanes flying overhead, birds
singing outside, appliances humming, and
so on. Experience each sound fully.
Allow it to pass through you.

Now imagine that your ears are extremely
sensitive antennae. Extend your listening out
farther and farther into physical space. Can you
hear the sounds of a highway some distance away?
The sound of an appliance in another part of the
house? The sounds of the airport 20 miles away?

The sound of a river 100 miles away? The sound of the ocean 200 miles away? The sounds of a city 1000 miles away? And so on. Keep pushing out the boundaries of what you can hear. There are no limits. Become immersed in the sounds.

After you end the exercise, record your experiences.

As a variation, you can start this exercise out-of-doors and focus on the sounds of nature. Hear the obvious sounds. Then, as you extend your sensitivity, listen for the softer and more subtle sounds of nature: the rustling of small animals and birds in bushes, leaves rustling in trees, insects crawling through blades of grass, the sound of clouds moving through the sky, the sound of things growing.

LISTENING TO THE INNER WORLD

As before, use the three-step breath technique on page 56 to enter into a meditative state with your eyes closed. Become aware of the sounds of your environment. Allow them to pass through you.

Now turn your attention inward. Listen carefully to the sound of your breathing. Become totally immersed in the sound.

Go deeper. Hear your heartbeat. Listen to your digestion. Then go deeper still to hear the blood rushing through the veins and arteries. Go deeper still. Hear the sounds of cells doing their jobs to keep your physical house functioning. Listen for the impulses of brain activity.

Go deeper still, deep into the interior of your being, where you hear the sound of the cosmic currents of being.

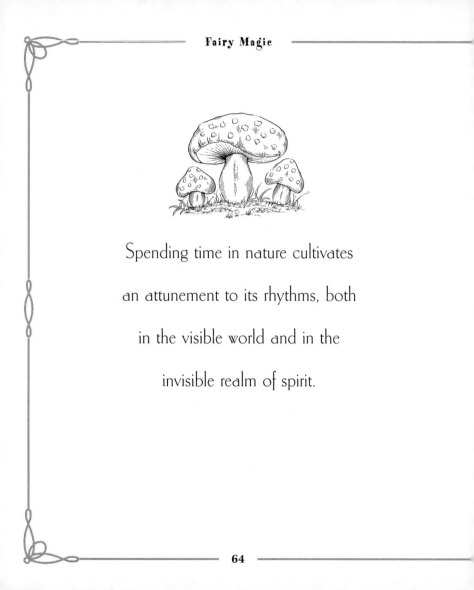

Spending time in nature cultivates

an attunement to its rhythms, both

in the visible world and in the

invisible realm of spirit.

Record your experiences. Did any sounds surprise you?

Riding the Waves

This exercise will advance your ability to extend your consciousness outward into the environment around you. Tape record the guided meditation and play it during your meditation, or have a friend read the script to help you enter the experience. This exercise can be done in a group as well.

Use the three-step breath technique on page 56 to enter into a meditative state of consciousness.

Imagine yourself at the seashore. Stand with bare feet at the water's edge. Watch the waves roll in

and lap the beach. Smell the salt air. Feel
the crunch of the sand beneath your feet.
Hear the sound of the waves, the cries of shore
birds. The ocean stretches into infinity.

Notice that the sunlight falling upon the water
makes the surface sparkle like millions of gems.
You are warm, happy and content. You are
fully present to the moment. There is no past,
no tomorrow, only the eternal moment.

Focus your attention on the action of the
waves. The water rolls in, the water rolls out.
Timeless, eternal motion.

Imagine that your consciousness flows out
from you in waves of energy. See the waves
rippling from you. Synchronize the waves of your
consciousness with the ocean waves. Let yourself

become lighter and lighter. Your body begins to change into waves of energy. Become lighter still, until you are only energy. Flow out over the ocean waves.

Now you are a wave of energy riding along the waves of the ocean. Feel the flow, the surge and ebb. The tide is going out. Allow yourself to be carried along with it, easily, gently. You are filled with complete peace and harmony, at one with the sparkling ocean. You feel energized. The ocean is the universe. You are one with the currents of the universe.

The currents carry you out and out. Here you are free of distraction. Here you are free of limitation. You can know the answers to all questions. You can know all things.

A message is given to you. The spirits of the
ocean bestow it upon you. Perhaps they have
a bird cry it out. Perhaps they write it in the
clouds in the sky. Perhaps it wells up within you.

Give thanks for your message. Know that
it is right for you.

When you feel ready, return to awareness
of your physical body.

Record your experience and your impressions.

In the Flow

All things in the universe are composed of energy.
The energy can assume any form, and can become

organized into patterns, such as the physical realm. Matter is energy. Consciousness is energy. Our thoughts and feelings are energy. Creativity is energy. Intuition is energy. The essence of the soul is energy.

The energies of the universe are in constant motion and interplay. As energies affect each other, they change form. In this exercise, we will change the form of our energy, transmuting the body, which has limitations, into waves of energy, which have no limit. As a wave of energy, you can more easily experience the fairy realm.

Tape the following guided meditation script or have a friend read it to you. Use the three-step breath technique on page 56 to help you relax and centre.

Imagine yourself floating down a gentle river. Notice that the water is golden. The sunlight

falling upon it makes the surface sparkle like millions of golden gems. You are warm, happy and content, floating easily down the river. You are fully present to the moment. There is no past, no tomorrow, only the eternal moment.

The gems sparkle and flash. The river of water becomes a river of light.

As you float along in the river of light, become aware of your body. It begins to change. See yourself being filled by the golden light of the sun, and by the sparkles from the river. The light transforms you, turning you into a golden being. You become lighter and lighter. You see that the golden light that is now you is actually comprised of millions of sparkling golden gem lights, just like the sunlight dancing on the water of the river.

Allow yourself to sink deeper and deeper into this
field of sparkling lights. You feel energized.
Suddenly you realize that you are one and the
same with the river of light.

Feel the flow of the motion of light. Allow
yourself to be carried along with it. You are
filled with complete peace and harmony,
at one with the light.

Up ahead you see a round, golden ball of light.
It is the Source of All Being, the supply of
universal good. The river of light is flowing
into it. A cosmic river merging into a
cosmic sun. The river flows effortlessly
into it, merging perfectly with it.

Feel yourself merging with cosmic energy. It
becomes part of you, and you become part of it.
You cannot be separated from it. Stay in this space
for a few moments, and notice how you feel.

When you feel ready, return to an awareness of
your physical body. As you feel more solid, know
that the light remains within you.

The rewards of practice

Do any of these exercises at least three times a
week. What changes do you notice in how you look
at things? Do you have a new and different appreciation of detail? Do you observe details that you did
not before? Can you notice nature spirits?

You may suddenly find yourself able to shift and expand your consciousness at will, so that you can attune quickly to whatever environment you are in. Marvellous experiences with fairies can unfold.

I had an interesting experience at a fairy lake in Wales by using these techniques of extending my senses. The experience was particularly significant because it was shared with a friend. Unbeknownst to each other, we had identical visionary experiences independent of each other. The fact that we experienced the same details validated the experience for both of us.

On a windy, foggy and rainy autumn day, Jo and I took a trip to Llyn y Fan Fach (pronounced *chlinnuh van vach*), a remote lake in the Black Mountains near the hamlet of Myddfai. The lake is known for its water fairy, the Lady of the Lake.

According to the lore, a young man is at the lake one day when a beautiful water fairy maiden rises up out of its waters. Smitten, he desires to marry her. Her father consents, and gives her a fine dowry of cattle. He places one condition upon his son-in-law: that he never strike his daughter or touch her with iron. If he does so three times, she will return to the lake forever.

The two marry and have four sons. They are very happy, but over the course of time the husband forgets himself and strikes his wife. He does not give her blows, but taps her. The first time, he gives her a light tap to hurry her along when she is late. The second time, he tries to stop her from crying at a wedding. The third time, he tries to stop her from laughing at a funeral.

Upon the third tap, she takes all of her cattle and they all disappear forever back into the lake. But before she goes, she teaches her fairy arts of healing to her sons. They become the sires of a long line of respected physicians. Myddfai becomes known for its physicians, and also for its fair maidens.

This story appears in different versions for other fairy-haunted lakes, and for other tales of fairy and human inter-marriage.

The day we visited Myddfai and the lake, the elementals provided an appropriately mysterious atmosphere. The fog hung low over the mountain peaks and the wind made thin screaming sounds. What secrets were shrouded in the mists?

From the car park, we had a 20-minute hike along a path up into the hills. We passed through three gates along the way. Three is the number of magic, as in three wishes, and as we passed through the third gate we seemed to cross a threshold into a weirdly parallel realm. We were the only humans about, and as we got higher up, even the sheep vanished.

When we finally reached the lake – which has been dammed and is now more of a reservoir – we were both disappointed and thrilled. We were disappointed because the fog had become so low and thick that we could not see across to the opposite shore. In fact, we could barely see the coastline for more than a few hundred yards. There was only a wall of grey, the hint of shorelines, and the sound of unseen water being whipped by the wind. We were thrilled because the place seemed at once otherworldly and mysterious – the very kind of place where one would encounter beings from another realm.

Ignoring our discomfort at being wet and cold, Jo and I sat down on rocks a short distance apart from each other to do our own meditations. I entered into a state of mindfulness and expanded my consciousness to be in harmony with the environment.

Presently, I became aware of a new sound coming through the greyness. The wind-whipped water had shifted to the sounds of a boat moving along the surface. There was a slap-slap-slap sound of waves hitting wood. Then I had a vision of a grey-white vessel with a high prow emerging out of the fog. It was old, medieval, timeless. It seemed to be coming toward me, but it never got any closer to shore. And then it dissolved back into the mists.

At first I wanted to dismiss the experience, for it seemed like something I would *like* to experience: the ferry of the lake fairies. However, I knew my prior experience to trust what I had sensed. I discovered that Jo had had the same experience – the same sounds and the same vision. She, too, had wondered about it before accepting it.

As we walked around the shoreline, my head was flooded with ideas of a creative nature. Whatever had transpired triggered something within me. It was a gift from the fairy realm. I always carry a little notebook with me, and I recorded the details of the experience and the ideas.

The following chapters present techniques for establishing and refining communication with fairies. We will graduate from passive receptivity to pro-active contact.

4

Fairy Care

Fairies work quietly around us. Unless we are born with marked clairvoyant ability or we develop second sight through study and exercises such as those given in this book, we are not likely to notice fairies. Many of them prefer to remain distant from our world, too, and so take steps to avoid direct contact with us. But many fairies readily make themselves known to us, when we ask with sincerity. These fairies have taken on the roles of bridge-building between our world and theirs.

Fairies take a great deal of pride in their work and in their role in the scheme of all things. They like to be treated respectfully and have their contributions recognized and rewarded. Fairies who feel appreciated will more than go the distance to help you. But criticize them or let them feel neglected or taken for granted and they will be quick to let you know they are upset by stirring up a little disorder in your world. Unhappy household fairies, for example, have been known to break dishes, turn over objects, create messes and hide things.

Show your appreciation by creating or recognizing special places for fairies in your house or on your land, and by leaving small offerings of food, drink and trinkets. They are especially fond of sweets, cream and milk, and shiny objects. Don't leave money, however. Many household fairies will work tirelessly in exchange for appreciation, food and other small offerings, but will take offence at being paid like a labourer. Some will even depart in a huff, and you may have a difficult time coaxing them to return.

Above all, be careful about iron objects. Fairies do not like iron, for it saps their strength and repels them. Do not use iron implements in your garden, and keep iron objects away from areas in your home where you feel a fairy presence.

Fairies have a great sense of humour, and they enjoy their play and leisure time. Some of them delight in tricks. You may not mind a fairy having an occasional laugh at your expense, but don't indulge fairies at home who like excessive trickery. Be polite but stern and ask them to go; then find other lodgers. (We will be talking more about this in Chapter 6.)

Fairies who feel appreciated will more

than go the distance to help you.

Fairy nooks

Everyone has a special place at home that is 'theirs', even if it is only a favourite chair for reading or watching television. Perhaps you are fortunate enough to have a small sacred space for meditation.

Fairies like to have special places in homes to call their own, too. They will find their own nooks where they are most comfortable. But they are also appreciative of special places you set aside for them. It's a sign to them that you are mindful of their wellbeing and wish them to be a full participant in the household.

Your household fairy will make it known to you where the best place is in your home for a fairy nook. Follow your intuition or ask your dreams to show you. Generally, fairies like places where they can survey rooms, and where they are out of the main household traffic and areas where guests are entertained. Bookshelves and tables in corners and alcoves are favourites.

My own fairy nook is in what I call the 'Angel Garden Room'. It is on the ground floor of my home, with a window that looks out onto the backyard. The room is decorated in greens, roses and whites with floral chintz, and it has many images and figurines of angels and fairies. It is a restful, peaceful place, and I like to meditate there.

The focal point on my white bookshelf in the Angel Garden Room is a pewter fairy figurine standing on a lily pad. The figurine is large, and the lily pad is meant to serve as a tray. I place things on the lily pad for the household fairy: small offerings of sweets, crystals, flowers, and so forth.

Fairies appreciate being acknowledged. When you are near their nook, or are coming to leave something for them, greet them and inquire how they are getting along. You needn't speak out loud; fairies will pick up on your thoughts.

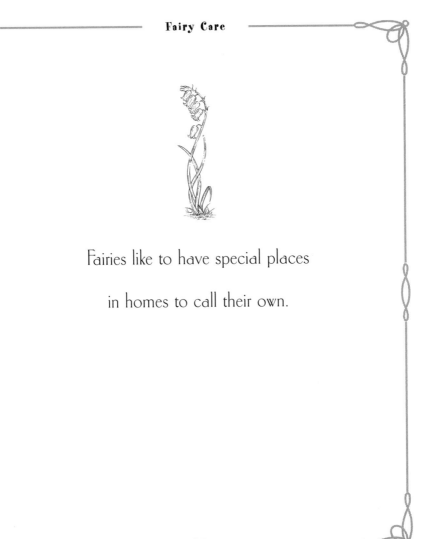

Fairies like to have special places

in homes to call their own.

Fairy altars

In addition to a fairy nook, you may wish to set up a fairy altar. Altars are important in spiritual work, for they represent the meeting place of heaven and earth. The altar opens a door to spiritual realms. A fairy altar can serve as both a place to leave gifts for household fairies, and also a place to conduct fairy magic.

Small accent tables and boxes make excellent altars, and can be set up in a corner of your bedroom or a quiet area of the house. If you do not have space for a permanent altar, you can keep your altar objects in a special box and get them out whenever you wish to do a ritual.

For your fairy altar, you will want to have on hand both basic and personal objects. The basics are:

✦ A cloth to cover the altar top. If your space is small, use a pretty cloth napkin or handkerchief. Green is always a favourite colour of fairies. Green awakens the heart centre, and is a colour of balance and healing as well.

✦ Representatives of the four elements. A candle serves for fire, incense or a feather serve for air, a stone, crystal or dish of salt serve for earth, a shell or a small dish of water serve for water. Having symbols of the four elements represents being in balance with the natural world, and invites the spirits of the elements to be present.

✦ Devotional objects. These include religious objects, images, statues and symbols, as well as objects of personal significance that foster your connection to the Divine. Devotional objects symbolize connection to the spiritual realms.

My own altar objects are quite eclectic: an angel pin, a small figurine of a lake fairy on a lily pad, a small card with an image of Madonna and Child, a small Goddess figurine, saint medallions, written magical charms, a silver medallion inscribed with 42 names of God in Hebrew, and a cross.

✦ Objects such as stones collected from special places (and always with permission).

Having an altar space at home serves as the 'meeting place' with fairies and also with angels.

Altars are important in spiritual work,

for they represent the meeting place

of heaven and earth.

Fairy stones

Your personal relationship with fairies can be further strengthened by carrying on your person a stone or special object associated with the fairy realm. Perhaps you're already in the habit of carrying or wearing a lucky charm. Objects believed to be lucky, or to have special protective powers against misfortune, have a long history. These objects help the owner to connect with the forces of spirit and nature and bring favourable powers into play for them.

Stones and crystals have a particularly strong connection to the fairy realm. Holed stones especially are associated with lucky, protective and healing powers. A fairy stone carried or worn will constantly energize your connection to fairies.

A personal fairy stone is not the same as the one or ones you place on your fairy altar, for it should be kept on or close to the body. Keep it in a pocket or purse, or wear it on a chain, cord or charm bracelet. Let it remind you of the ever-present workings of the fairy realm wherever you go.

Select a fairy stone by asking the fairies to show it to you. You will know the right one as soon as you see it and handle it – a special feeling will be conveyed to you through your intuition. You may find it in your own garden, or perhaps when you visit a special place. Your fairy stone also may be a crystal – or even a gem – that you find in a shop.

You may be drawn to other objects as special fairy charms, such as shells. Stones and crystals (and gems) are the best, however. They are durable, and their earthiness establishes a powerful link to the invisible dimension of the natural world.

A fairy stone carried or worn

will constantly energize your

connection to fairies.

5

Building Communication with Fairies

It's surprisingly easy to communicate with fairies, especially once you have opened your fairy sight. Here are ways to build your relationship with the fairy realm.

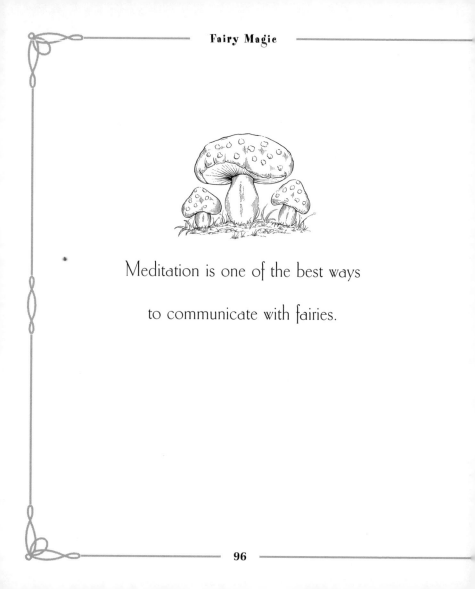

Meditation is one of the best ways

to communicate with fairies.

Meditation

As we have already seen, meditation is one of the best ways to communicate with fairies. A meditative state of consciousness helps you to achieve the expanded vision and listening attunement that brings the fairy realm into focus.

Meditate in fairy nooks and places where fairies are said to frequent. If you ask inwardly to be guided to the right places, you will feel a gentle tug in the proper direction. Trust the guidance.

Close your eyes and imagine that a cloud of loving energy in sparkling rainbow hues surrounds you. Expand the cloud out to the surrounding environment. Invite the fairies – or a specific fairy – to enter this protected space.

Take note of the impressions and thoughts that arise spontaneously within you. If you like, ask specific questions. The answers will be given inwardly, or through signs in the outer environment. Answers may not appear immediately, but later at a more appropriate time, or when certain props are available to the fairies.

Fairy presence is always strong in sacred places. Whenever I have the chance to visit a sacred site, I make time for meditation. The presences of place can include gods and angels as well as fairies. You never know what will come through when you invite the invisible residents to make themselves known.

I had a lovely and rather unexpected visitation from a fairy when I visited the Roman ruins of a hilltop dream healing temple at Lydney, Gloucestershire, between the Forest of Dean and the River Severn.

Once this sacred place attracted thousands who came in the hope that through their dreams they would meet the god Nodens, who would heal them as they slept. Many went away healed.

Lydney has several sites of Roman ruins, including one of the most important Roman archaeological sites in all of Britain: a camp and temple at Lydney Park believed to be the cult shrine of Sabrina, goddess of the Severn. The ruins of the dream temple are on privately owned land and are open to the public for brief periods every year. Because of its remote location and private ownership, the site retains a wild, quiet and pristine atmosphere that may not be much different than it was during the Roman occupation of Britain.

The Romans built the Lydney healing temple in the late fourth century AD. Their healing temples were inspired by the dream healing temples of the Greeks, who believed strongly in dreams as a medium of contact with the gods. The Lydney temple was on a much smaller scale than some of the grand Greek dream temples, but it offered a complete healing sanctuary: a temple for the priests; a hydrotherapy centre of Roman-style cold, warm and hot baths; a dream dormitory or abaton; and stalls for resident physicians, consultants and healers.

The Greek temples were dedicated to their primary god of dream healing, Aesculapius. Lydney was not dedicated to a major deity, but to a little-known deity, Nodens. The Romans were great adapters, and Nodens was derived from a Celtic deity: the Welsh Nudd of the Silver Hand (and Lludd, the namesake of Ludgate in London) and the Irish Nuada of the Silver Hand. Nodens/Nudd was a water deity, and it is thought that the Severn River itself was his silver arm and hand.

To get to the temple ruins, one crosses a small stream – a symbol of a portal crossing into another realm or world – and then one climbs a steep and winding hill. Magnificent trees, including oaks and beeches, line the route.

As I started my journey at the base of the hill, I tried to send my consciousness back two thousand years to experience what it must have been like when the sacred temple was at its glory. I had heard that Nodens is still an active presence at the site – for those who are respectful and seek to make contact. I also had heard that the fairy presence was quite strong there, too.

I was fortunate to have the site all to myself and my travelling companion. Too often, the coming and going of spectators disturb fragile energy. (In fact, it is almost impossible to tune in to the otherworld at some of the most popular sacred sites that are overrun with tourists.) After experiencing the ruins and walking about the grounds, I was attracted to a huge oak tree whose gnarled roots poked above the surface of the ground. The tree itself seemed to be a portal between worlds. I sat down against it and entered into a meditative state with my eyes open.

The stillness of the afternoon penetrated me. I expanded my field of consciousness into the environment. I had no expectations. Would I meet Nodens? Would I encounter fairies? Or would I simply have a pleasant, drifting meditation? I did not know, but I resolved to be open.

After a while, I suddenly became aware that I was being regarded by a small figure who had material-ized by the tree. It seemed that he – for it was a masculine presence – came out of the roots of the tree. His clothing was not distinct, but I could clearly make out the vivid red cap on his head. He seemed old, like a little old man, and I had the impression of grey whiskers or beard. I would guess his height at about two feet. He seemed curious about me more than anything. I knew he wanted me to see him and acknowledge him, for if he had wished to watch me in secrecy he could have easily done so.

I gave him a mental greeting and thanked him for joining me. I received a mental impression of a greeting in return, and his appreciation of my respect for the place. He stayed for a bit, and then suddenly he was gone. I had the impression that he disappeared back down the tree roots.

Many fairy contacts are similar to this: they reveal themselves for the sole purpose of making themselves known and experienced, as a validation of their presence in the world.

My experience at Lydney had many benefits, including healing and new creativity. Meditating at any place where you sense the palpable presence of spirit – whether it be a known sacred site or just a place you come upon – can have amazing results.

Meditation helps you to achieve

the expanded vision and listening

attunement that brings the fairy

realm into focus.

Automatic Drawing

The fairy realm communicates in images and intuitive impressions, which say far more than words. We receive mental pictures and impressions that are translated into words by our own thought processes. Automatic drawing can establish a powerful link with the fairy realm. You needn't be a skilled artist to receive a vivid image. If you're trusted, fairies will enjoy sending you impressions of their portraits.

When I visited Findhorn, I met individuals who had impressive portfolios of fairy portrait transmissions. One man initiated his process by tuning in to Findhorn's Landscape Angel. He found himself spontaneously drawing a portrait of the angel, all the while feeling the powerful presence of this being as he drew. The drawing process itself was spontaneous and fluent, requiring no corrections nor any preparation or pre-drawing of the design. Each dot found its proper place and the image built up in front of me in such a way that I only knew what was being drawn when the completed image appeared on the paper. This was equally true for each drawing he made.

A woman whom I shall call Cynthia likened the automatic drawing process to faxing: the fairies, she said, had chosen her as a kind of fax machine to receive images intended to strengthen the relationship between humanity and the nature kingdom.

'What is impinged on my mind I draw, not knowing what I am drawing,' she said. 'I do not "see" nature spirits or devas, though I do feel their presence before and during drawing them. I am always alone before and during drawing, in a peaceful, contented mood with an "empty" mind. Stillness is essential. Nature beings home in on me. It is their choice – they want to be drawn. I am only the available mind and hand.'

Cynthia received validation of what she drew. For example, she showed R. Ogilvie Crombie a drawing she had made of a spirit during a visit to Findhorn Foundation. Crombie had talked about 'the Sand Goblin', but had never described its appearance. He looked at Cynthia's drawing and said, 'You have drawn what I see.'

Cynthia told me, 'My function is to show the reality of the beings and tell their story. The unseen beings come to be expressed in a humanistic form – for they can appear in many forms – so that humans can recognize their existence and visualize them, love them and ask for their cooperation and wisdom.

The nature kingdom longs to work with humans, and needs help and cooperation to bring about awareness and change of our whole attitude to them – our needs against our greed.

'The destructive influences must be balanced so that a perfect cosmic evolution can emerge. Beauty and harmony need to be restored to our beloved planet. The shining, beautiful devas and nature spirits long to work with us. They are here for us all to invite them. Please do, whether you have a whole forest or just a plant on your table. Make a beginning!'

Here is how you can make your own beginning with automatic fairy drawing:

1. Centre yourself in meditation.
2. Ask for the fairy who wishes to have its portrait drawn.

3. Begin drawing. If nothing seems clear immediately, make flowing, free-form lines until an image takes shape. You will feel the energy shift; you may wish to change to fresh paper when this occurs.

4. Trust the image you receive. Do not try to make it conform to preconceived ideas or other images you have seen of fairies. Forms may not necessarily be humanistic – they can also be swirling shapes of colours.

5. Ask for a name or other identity.

6. Save your drawings in a special notebook or portfolio.

Automatic drawing can establish a

powerful link with the fairy realm.

Fairy conversation

Fairy conversation is a combination of the spoken word and mental impressions. Speak to your invisible friends as though they are physically present. Talk to them as you would your human friends. Fairies appreciate politeness, courtesy and a respectful tone, but you needn't be stiff and formal. They will answer you with mental impressions. You may not hear distinct words, but rather get 'whole' impressions.

Practise the expanded listening techniques described in Chapter 3 to improve your ability to recognize and understand subtle impressions.

Talk to fairies as you would

your human friends.

Dreams

We can ask angels to give us guidance and answers to questions in dreams. We can ask fairies, too. Like angels, fairies have the ability to navigate different realms, including the dreamscape. When we dream, we are free of the limitations of time and space, and our dreams become interdimensional meeting places.

I have done dreamwork for the better part of my life, and I believe that dreams are one of our best and richest sources of spiritual, creative and practical guidance. Dreams deliver powerful messages and great ideas.

We all dream nightly, and we have multiple dreams throughout our sleep cycle. Most of us remember only the dream we are having prior to waking up.

Some people naturally have sharper dream recall than others. Some have a difficult time remembering dreams, and may think they do not dream at all. However, scientific research has demonstrated that we do dream, whether we remember them or not. We can improve our ability to remember dreams and more details in dreams by paying attention to them.

Many people disregard their dreams because on the surface they seem rather strange and inscrutable. Yet dreams reveal themselves quite easily when we catch on to how they communicate. Dreams speak in symbols. They convey impressions.

If you ask the fairy realm for information to be given to you in dreams, you will be following an ancient and honoured tradition of 'dream incubation'. Your request is incubated in dreaming, and something new is born from it. The ancient dream temples such as Lydney, described at the beginning of this chapter, were places of dream incubation for healing.

Pilgrims to the dream temples prepared themselves for meeting the gods in their dreams. Similarly, you will have the best results if you prepare yourself mentally and physically. You won't need to make major changes to your daily life. Dream incubation is simple.

Set aside a day and evening for the incubation. In the morning and throughout the day, think about the question you plan to ask. Eat lightly, especially in the evening, for heavy meals, alcohol and stimulants can disrupt the sleep cycle and make dream recall more difficult.

Prior to bedtime, relax with inspirational reading. Lighting a candle or burning incense adds to the sensory pleasure of the ritual and heightens your anticipation. Write down your question on a slip of paper and place it beneath your pillow. For example, if you are trying to decide whether or not to take a certain course of action, ask 'Should I _____?'

If you need help accomplishing something, ask 'How can I _____?'

or

'Where will I find the help I need to _____?'

Ask the fairy realm – or a particular fairy – to help you understand the answer in your dreams. Put your fairy stone or charm beneath your pillow, too. Be sure to give thanks for getting the answer.

If you use an alarm, set it a little earlier than usual. You will want to have adequate time to record your dream after you awaken. Recording it is very important, as dreams are quickly forgotten. One method I use is to repeat the dream to myself silently before I get up, which helps to set it into my memory. Then I write it down along with my associations and ideas about its meaning. Later, when I have more time, I return to the written account and work with it again.

Record your dream and work with it even if it does not seem to obviously answer your question. The answer may be couched in layers of symbolism. There may be no obvious 'fairy' in the dream. Fairies and angels make use of our natural intuition and the symbolic language of dreams to impress information and messages upon us.

You may have a dream that vividly answers the question. Or, you may not remember a dream, but you will know the answer upon awakening. This often happens to me. I wake up with the answer crystal clear in my mind. Sometimes the answer comes in a dream a night or two later. Answers also come in synchronicities experienced in the day. Watch for any special fairy signs you already recognize.

If you feel you haven't received an answer, try again. If you still feel you haven't received an answer after three tries, try rewording the question. Sometimes we put the cart before the horse, especially when we're looking for solutions to problems. Re-examine your dreams to make certain you didn't overlook the answer.

Fairies will give you guidance

and answers to your questions

in your dreams.

Fairy stone dowsing

Have you ever tried dowsing with a pendulum? The pendulum – such as a crystal, stone or metal cylinder suspended on a cord – is a popular tool for activating the intuitive/psychic sense. It has been used for thousands of years in dowsing, which is a form of divination for locating lost and missing persons and animals, and for detecting hidden objects and substances, such as water, oil, coal, minerals, cables and pipes. Dowsing also is used in the mapping of archaeological sites. Many people dowse as a way of asking about decisions and choices for virtually any purpose.

Ask the fairies to help you select a dowsing stone – you will intuitively be drawn to the right one. Ideally, it should be small and fairly uniform in shape, so that it hangs in a well-balanced way from a cord. Tie the stone onto a cord or string about six to eight inches in length. Use it as a pendulum for dowsing. Hold the cord between your thumb and forefinger and allow the stone to hang straight and still. It will move of its own accord in answer to questions.

First you must establish how the stone communicates yes and no. Hold the pendulum steady and ask, 'Give me a yes.' Do not try to stimulate movement. Allow it to respond naturally. After a few moments, the pendulum will begin to rotate or swing back and forth. The more vigorous the motion, the stronger the response. Stop the pendulum and hold it steady again. Ask, 'Give me a no.' Allow the pendulum to respond naturally again.

Most likely, the no will be the opposite motion of the yes. For example, if the pendulum rotates clockwise for yes, it probably will rotate counter clockwise for no.

Ask the pendulum a series of yes and no questions to which you know the answers. This will firmly establish the response pattern of the pendulum.

You can use your fairy stone pendulum to ask questions directly to the fairy realm, and also ask fairies to assist in the dowsing process.

Acknowledging the fairy presence

Do at least one of these communication bridge-builders every day, or as often as possible. Even a short meditation of a few minutes will have a beneficial effect. You may not immediately be aware of a response, but your efforts will not go unnoticed. You will get responses at the appropriate times. With more and more practice, you will have an increasingly easy time tuning in to the realm of fairy.

6
Tricks and Trouble

Fairies – especially household ones – have a keen sense of humour and they like to play tricks, even when they're not upset with you. Being a bit of a trickster is in their nature. If you are going to develop a relationship with them, you must be prepared to deal with this side of their nature. Most of the jokes they play on humans are benign and carry no serious

consequences, though we may be mightily annoyed
for a time. If you learn to go along in a good-
humoured way with a joke on yourself every now
and then, you will get along well with fairies – and
you probably will find fewer and fewer tricks
played on you as time goes on.

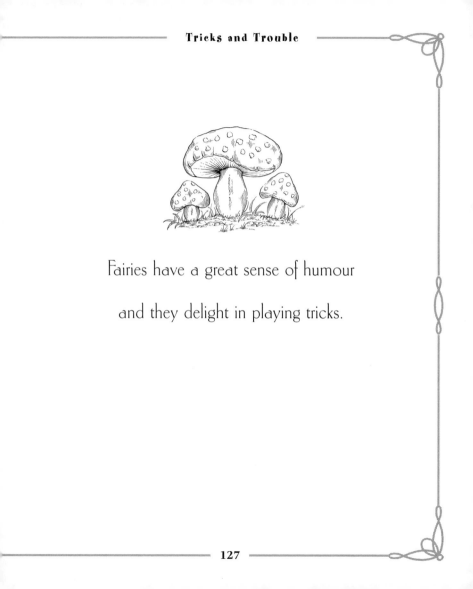

Fairies have a great sense of humour

and they delight in playing tricks.

Missing objects

One of the fairies' favourite tricks is to hide things. They may 'borrow' something just when you go looking for it, and then watch gleefully while you steam about searching in vain. They'll return it, but often in some unlikely location.

In parapsychology, the study of paranormal phenomena, the mysterious disappearance and reappearance of objects is called 'jotts', an acronym for 'just one of those things'. The acronym was coined by Mary Rose Barrington, a psychical researcher and officer of the Society for Psychical Research in London. Jotts are a fascinating area of study. Possible explanations that have been put forward are teleportation or some sort of spontaneous psychokinesis. I think we must also consider the meddlings of fairies as a possibility. Fairies are quite capable of moving between worlds, and they possess the knowledge of cosmic forces to move objects from our realm with them.

There are different categories of jotts, or 'jottles', as they are also known:

Walkabout. An article disappears from a known location and is found later in another and often bizarre location, without explanation for how it got there.

Comeback. An article disappears from a known location and later – sometimes minutes or perhaps even years – mysteriously reappears in the same location. It may be a special case of walkabout.

Flyaway. An article disappears from a known location and never reappears. Flyaways may be stage 1 of a walkabout with an exceptionally long time-frame.

Turn-up. An article known to an observer but from an unknown location is found in a place where it was previously known to be. Turn-ups may be stage 2 of a walkabout.

Windfall. A turn-up in which an article is not known to the observer.

Trade-in. A flyaway followed by a windfall that is closely similar to the article flown away.

Walkabouts are the most common of the fairy jottles, and usually involve small objects. You look for something in a location where you know you last saw it or placed it, only to find that it isn't there. At first you think you've just forgotten where it is, but an increasingly thorough search turns up nothing. It's true that sometimes our memory is faulty and we *think* we know where an object is but we are mistaken. Nonetheless, there are many times when the disappearance of an object is simply unexplained and mysterious.

Sometimes the object reappears in exactly the spot where we first looked for it, and we wonder how on earth we could have missed it. Sometimes it turns up in a strange location – a place where we would not normally leave the object.

When things are taken on walkabouts, they usually don't stay away long. But if the fairies are angry or mean-spirited, they may stage a flyaway, in which something disappears for a very long time, perhaps even for good.

The solution to a walkabout is to ask the fairies to return the object promptly to a place where you will find it: 'All right, you've had your fun. Now may I please have my ring back?' or 'I'm in need of my book, so please return it now.' Getting angry is likely to only make the fairies more stubborn.

In certain cases, the fairies will make a substitution when they do a return. Trade-ins are things of comparable or better value than the original objects lost. The fairies may covet the thing they took and be unwilling to give it up, or they may be genuinely trying to do you a good turn by giving you something they think you will like better. You can always ask for the original object to be restored, but you will probably have to accept the trade-in.

Sometimes fairies do a good turn by providing a windfall – a desirable object that turns up without warning. You may think it's luck, but probably there's a fairy behind it!

If walkabouts happen frequently to you and to the point where you are truly annoyed and seriously inconvenienced, firmly tell the fairies that they must stop this mischievous behaviour, because it is harmful to you. Ask them why – they may have a complaint that needs to be remedied, such as an object harmful to them near their fairy nook or altar.

Messes and disorder

Another common trick of fairies is to create messes and disorder. Things will fall off shelves and tables and break. Clutter will suddenly appear. Tools will be found in disarray.

Messiness is usually a sign that fairies are unhappy about something in their environment. You've interfered with their work, or you've neglected them, or you've done something they consider disrespectful. Once the fences are mended with them, order will be restored.

Apologies go a long way with fairies. The relationship should not be one-sided, however. You should let them know when you're unhappy with them as well. Set good boundaries and ground rules of mutual respect and cooperation.

Messiness is usually a sign that fairies

are unhappy about something in

their environment.

Troublesome fairies

Sometimes fairies are bad-tempered, just like some people. If one or more of those has taken up residence in your house, they must be told to leave. Remove objects and stones associated with the offenders. Do a ritual cleansing of the fairy spaces with incense and a lit candle. Tell the unwanted negative energies to depart and invite in positive energies. For example, as you take your candle and incense to every room of the house, say out loud in a firm voice, 'Your presence is not welcome here and you are to depart immediately. Go with blessings, but do not return.'

Fairy lore is full of particular fairies and types of fairies who are not kindly disposed towards people. There are malevolent ones who like to lure people into trouble or even to their deaths, such as fairies who live in certain watery areas and in deep woods. It's not likely that they will bother you, especially if you are respectful of the environment wherever you go. Establishing a pleasant relationship with the fairy realm also will impart an aura around you that will identify you as 'fairy friendly' to unknown ones you encounter.

Once you have gained the

confidence and trust of fairies,

they increase their interactions

with you.

I

Working with Fairies

Once you have gained the confidence and trust of fairies, they increase their interactions with you. They appreciate honesty, openness, straightforwardness, generosity, kindness and thoughtfulness. When they see these traits and behaviours in humans, they respond in kind and bestow their special gifts upon them as well.

Traditionally, fairies are known for certain special gifts: luck and prosperity; healing; skill in crafts, and skill in the arts. In addition, the ones associated with the home help to maintain domestic harmony and order in all things, including the functioning of our tools, gadgets, appliances and equipment.

If you have done the skill-building exercises given earlier in this book, you will have established contact with fairies and will have learned more about them and your personal relationship to them. You will have developed your own unique ways of communicating with them, and you will have a sense of which fairies can be best approached for whatever need.

Here are general guidelines for different needs and tasks:

♦ **Earth fairies:** abundance in the material and physical worlds; luck; prosperity; finances; health; order; home and work; functioning of machines.

♦ **Air fairies:** study; intellectual pursuits; communication; ideas; inspirations; travel.

♦ **Water fairies:** healing work; emotional issues; personal happiness; love; dreams.

♦ **Fire fairies:** action; vitality; strength; perseverance; renewal; new beginnings; justice.

Once you have gained the

confidence and trust of fairies,

they increase their interactions

with you, and bestow their

special gifts upon you.

Thrice times the charm

In making requests of fairies, ask three times. Three is the number of creation and ascent, and opens the gateways to the higher planes. The number three plays a prominent role in myth, mysticism, folklore, alchemy, and the dynamics of spiritual growth and change. In the mystery traditions, numbers are not quantities. They are ideas or forms which constitute the building blocks of all things in the universe. Each number has it own vibration, character and attributes, which in turn influence the physical world by attracting certain energies.

The Greek philosopher Anatolius observed that three, 'the first odd number, is called perfect by some, because it is the first number to signify the totality – beginning, middle and end.' Thus, we find in mythology, folklore and fairy tales the recurrent motif of the triad: three wishes, three sisters, three brothers, three chances, blessings done in threes, and spells and charms done in threes ('thrice times the charm'). Three is also the number of wisdom and knowledge in its association with the Three Fates and the past, present and future, and the ancient sciences of music, geometry and arithmetic.

The fairy realm responds to the number three, and so repeat your formal requests three times. Do this if you are dowsing, or in meditation, or preparing for dream incubation – or in any situation where you feel that calling on fairy help will benefit you. For example, you might say, 'Help me manifest the love relationship that is right for me. Help me manifest the love relationship that is right for me. Help me manifest the love relationship that is right for me. Thrice times the charm, so be it.'

Whatever you ask for and receive, be sure to always give thanks for the help.

Luck and prosperity

As we saw in Chapter 1, fairies have long been associated with fertility and the abundance of the land. This was especially important in earlier times when most people earned their living from farming. Today most of us earn our living at a desk instead of on the land, but the symbolism of the luck of the land – and the luck that fairies bring – remains with us in the form of the rainbow. In fairy lore, a pot of gold lies at the end of the rainbow. In fairy tales, gold hunters never find the physical end of a rainbow. The lesson of the tales is that the gold lies within, not in the material world.

THE IMPORTANCE OF THE RAINBOW

The rainbow is a powerful symbol of abundance. In the Old Testament, it is a sign that God sits in the heavens to remind people of his covenant with them. In mythology, the rainbow is the path to heaven and the land of the gods. And, it is the bridge to higher consciousness guarded by angels, who in art are shown with rainbow wings.

To the idle, the rainbow is only a pretty sight, the symbol of wishful thinking. To the visionary, the rainbow represents optimism, hope and the attainment of dreams. The difference between wishful thinking and visionary thinking is action. Wishful thinking goes nowhere, but visionary thinking is the impetus for action that brings about desired change.

THE RAINBOW AS A TOOL

When your fairy sight has opened, you may see the auras of things in clouds, bands and swirls of rainbow colours. You may perceive fairies and devas themselves as patterns of rainbow colours. Geoffrey Hodson, an English clairvoyant and Theosophist, perceived devas and angels as flowing pillars and patterns of multi-hued light, rather than in the human-like form portrayed in lore.

I use the rainbow often in my own meditation and spiritual work with the angel and fairy realms. The rainbow is effective for changing consciousness and for accessing the invisible. I especially use it when I am asking for a boon and seeking help. Here's what to do:

In meditation, see a rainbow of light flowing
through you. It comes down from the heavens
and enters you through the top of your head.
It fills your body with wonderful light. See it
flowing through you and out into the earth.
It leaves the soles of your feet and radiates
down from your lower trunk. In this way, you
are connected to the higher planes and grounded
to the earth. You receive the inspiration and
nourishment from the spiritual realms, which
is processed in your body and aura. The flow
of light into the earth symbolizes your ability
to act and manifest in the material plane.

Feel light and buoyant. Become a living rainbow.
The light expands within you, and then expands
into the space around you. As you become
the rainbow light, affirm your abundance,
luck and prosperity.

This is excellent preparation that shifts consciousness to attune to the subtle energy patterns and presences of the fairy realm. It also sets your consciousness toward manifesting luck and good things.

From this state of consciousness, you can invoke the presence and help of a particular fairy or kind of fairy. Fairies have 'job descriptions' just as people do. Make specific requests for help.

Fairies have 'job descriptions'

just as people do.

Home fairies

Brownies and other home-based fairies appreciate – even demand – neatness, cleanliness and order. Some will not even consider going to a home that is unkempt and disorderly. They work to maintain order, and so do not like humans to constantly undo their efforts.

One needn't be fanatical about order, for homes are not museums, nor displays for photographs in fancy magazines. They're meant to be lived in and enjoyed. If you make a reasonable and consistent effort to keep your home well maintained, you can enjoy the presence of helpful home fairies.

Make a little nook or fairy altar for them, and formally invite them in. Make it clear that you expect friendly cooperation from them. Leave out small offerings of food – but don't make a show of it, for fairies are prideful and discreet. As we've seen in earlier chapters, they do not like to be hired outright. They consider their services gifts to be bestowed at their choosing.

The maintenance of home fairies helps to establish an overall atmosphere of harmony. Residents and visitors notice it – they feel relaxed and comfortable. Relationships can improve in this atmosphere. Even a healing force can be established.

Home fairies are especially good in dealing with clutter. Have you ever noticed how things just suddenly seem in disarray? Ask your home fairies help to keep things in their proper places.

Home fairies help to maintain

domestic harmony and order

in all things.

Fairies at work

The same things apply to fairies at work as they do in the home. Whatever the workplace, fairies like order and efficiency. Fairies can be invited into your workplace. Ask them to help maintain good communications and good relations, and to inspire creative ideas and solutions to problems. A small picture of a fairy or a green lucky charm hung or kept in a drawer can serve as the link to the fairy realm.

Machine devas

In earlier times, 'tool fairies' kept the working tools of the farmer or craftsman in good condition. Today our world is highly mechanized. Fairies have expanded their care to include our vehicles, appliances, office and home equipment and all things related to electronics and computers. I call these fairies the 'machine devas'.

Machine devas are especially elusive and prefer not to make direct contact with humans. However, we can establish a relationship with them by treating our mechanical devices and equipment with respect. If something does not function to your liking, don't heap abuse upon it. You will only alienate the machine devas and incur more problems. Expect things to work for you. Treat them with consideration. When the time comes to retire something, give thanks to the machine devas for the service they have rendered, and wish them well in re-establishing themselves in new mechanical homes.

Garden and nature fairies

The fairies who take care of gardens and the wild flora of nature have their attention entirely focused on nurturing plant essences. It is a complex task to help seeds germinate and plant life to grow. Everything – even a weed – is lavished with care and attention, for everything has its proper place and role in the grand scheme of creation.

Plants are sensitive to the energy emitted by the thoughts and emotions of people around them. If you have cared for plants with great attention to them and their wellbeing, you probably have experienced first-hand their sensitivity to their environment and caretakers.

This sensitivity was understood in the 19th century by George Washington Carver, an American agricultural chemist who developed the peanut and sweet potato into scores of independent products. Carver attributed his success to nothing more than loving and caring about his plants. When asked what secrets he possessed that could work such magic, he replied that anyone could do what he did: 'The secrets are in the plants. To elicit them you have to love them enough.'

In the early 20th century, American botanist Luther Burbank observed the same phenomena. Burbank once stated that he could make a plant grow according to his own design simply by willing his thoughts and love. Burbank said he developed the spineless cactus with his loving willpower, succeeding in getting them to breed out their thorns.

Studies have shown that plants possess auras that can be dowsed. They respond to human thought, emotion and intent, and the wellbeing or demise of other living things around them. Plants thrive in a background of classical music but suffer when rock and heavy metal is played.

In the 1960s, Cleve Backster, an American polygraph expert, attached the electrodes of a lie detector to the leaf of a draecena and observed that the plant appeared to respond in an emotional fashion when watered. It reacted to being burned and also only his *intent* to burn it.

Backster also found that plants could be sensitive to one particular person's heartbeat in a room filled with several people. Like Carver and Burbank, he concluded that plants are especially attuned to their caretakers and their moods. Positive thoughts and a happy mood are characteristics of 'green thumb' gardeners while anxiety, depression, or even a dislike of plants will produce poor growth.

Thoughts conveyed through prayer have been found to make flowers grow faster, taller and healthier-looking. Bernard Grad of McGill University in Montreal found that water held in the hands of a healer seemed to possess an energy that could increase the growth rate of budding barley seeds. These results also were obtained by two famous American healers, Ambrose and Olga Worrall, who used prayer at a distance to positively affect plant germination and growth.

As we saw earlier in the cases of Findhorn and similar garden communities, the ability of humans to interact with the consciousness of plants is facilitated by the fairies and devas who care for them. The fairies can see the intent in your heart. They know if you truly care about and love plants. The love energy that radiates from your heart is woven by the fairies into the energy fields of the plants.

Follow the examples set by Findhorn, Green Hope and Perelandra. Meditate to discover the needs of your plants. Ask the fairies for guidance in planting and caring for them. Whenever you intend to prune, cut and pull out, first inform the plants and their caretakers. Whenever you work with your plants, make sure you are in a positive frame of mind. Avoid gardening when upset, angry or depressed.

Fairies are drawn to stone circles, and like to congregate around them for revelry. Using fairy guidance, select stones to arrange in small circles in your flower beds.

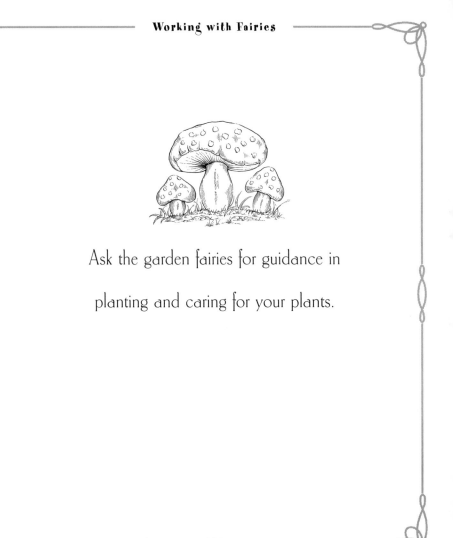

Ask the garden fairies for guidance in

planting and caring for your plants.

Healing

Garden fairies can be consulted for ways to bring out special healing properties in plants. Perhaps your particular home or location will benefit from the presence of certain plants. Perhaps there are certain fruits or vegetables you should cultivate. Shapes of beds, fertilizers, watering and combinations of plants in beds can influence the energetic properties of the plants and their flowers or produce.

In the wild, plant fairies will respond to your appreciation of nature. They will especially like the energy of your meditation. Spend time in natural settings and make contact with the fairy realm. The love and appreciation you send out carries a healing force that benefits the natural world.

Use the rainbow meditation on page 148 as a way of tuning in to the plant consciousness around you. On one occasion when I was out hiking in a wooded area, I sat down to meditate and visualized the rainbow of light flowing through me. Suddenly I experienced a shift of consciousness. The auras of the trees and plants were ablaze in pulsating swirls of rainbow colours of indescribable beauty. I was drawn the most to several trees near me, and it seemed that they communicated some of their 'life story' to me. I experienced an intuitive understanding of the spirit presences that took care of them – the fairies of the woodlands.

The healing energy that is raised in contact with nature can be sent out into the world. Visualize it travelling along a web of light that extends around the planet – a circuitry of energy.

Water fairies also are renowned for their healing gifts, as we saw in the lore of the lake maidens. Ask for their guidance, and for the bestowal of healing, in meditation by bodies of water. Running water – as in streams, rivers, falls and even fountains – is especially beneficial. If you do not live near a body of water, even a pond, buy a small table top fountain to keep in your house. The energy generated by running water is good for the overall health and harmony of the home.

Use the rainbow meditation, and also the Riding the Waves meditation described in Chapter 3.

Spend time in natural settings

and make contact with the fairy

realm. The love and appreciation

you send out carries a healing force

that benefits the natural world.

Skills and creativity

There are many stories in fairy lore of people receiving gifts of trade skills and in creative arts from fairies. Such gifts usually are given in gratitude for a good deed. In *The Fairy Faith in Celtic Countries*, W.Y. Evans-Wentz relates a legend from the Isle of Barra. The story goes that an apprentice carpenter was working with his master on a boat. He found he had forgotten a tool, and went back to his workshop to get it. There he disturbed a group of fairies who were working away in their own carpentry. The fairies ran, and one of them, a woman, dropped her little silk girdle in her haste. The boy picked it up and put it in his pocket. The fairy came out and asked for it back. He refused, and she promised that if he returned it, she would give him a master's skill immediately. The boy agreed and gave her back her girdle.

The next morning, the boy demonstrated such skill that his master recognized him as superior. The boy told him his secret, and for the rest of his life enjoyed a reputation as a superb master carpenter.

According to tradition, if you tell the secret of how you received your gift from the fairies, it vanishes immediately. But in this case, the boy kept his skill.

Robert Louis Stevenson credited brownies with inspiring him with story ideas in his dreams while he slept. He said they were present from childhood, and played in his dreams like little children on a stage. As he matured and became an author, the 'little people' became more trained and disciplined. The brownies laboured away all night, building story scenes and emotions.

Stevenson said his brownies played a major role in the creation of *Dr Jekyll and Mr Hyde*. 'I went about racking my brains for a plot of any sort,' he wrote. 'On the second night, I dreamed the scene at the window, and a scene afterward split in two in which Hyde, pursued for some crime, took the powder and underwent the change in the presence of his pursuers.' Stevenson awoke with the cry, 'I have it, that'll do!'

The brownies, he said, 'do one-half my work for me while I am fast asleep, and in all human likelihood, do the rest for me as well, when I am wide awake and fondly suppose I do it for myself.'

Dreams can be used to ask for fairy help for anything related to creativity, skills, talent, ideas and inspiration. Dreams also are effective for healing requests. Make your requests prior to sleep.

Lightweaving and gridwork

A more advanced work that can be done with the fairy realm involves patterns and flows of auric light. The effects of this are felt in the high, subtle realms that are sort of like a spiritual jet stream. The energies in this stream are constantly moving and shifting. They filter down like a gentle dew to the physical plane, where they are utilized by the thoughts, intent and actions of people to create events. This process goes on without the conscious awareness of most people.

Lightweaving and gridwork put more positive forces into motion. Energy that is more highly charged with love and spiritualized consciousness influences people for the better and encourages them to bring good, not darkness, into being.

Lightweaving and gridwork are governed by planetary fairies. They have a highly refined energy, and they route and marshal energies around a great grid that surrounds and penetrates the planet. Every living thing is hooked into the grid. Thus, we are all affected by the energies that move around the grid. The low energy of violence moves on this grid, as does the higher energy of love. The planetary fairies cannot prevent us from creating low energy. Their work is focused on maintaining harmony, order and balance, and we make it more difficult by the generation of low energy. By doing lightweaving and gridwork, we increase the positive forces that can neutralize and defeat low energy. The energy of lightweaving and gridwork goes where it is needed, and we may not see any immediate results. We must trust the process.

Lightweaving is directed at mental and spiritual consciousness, and gridwork is directed at the physical plane.

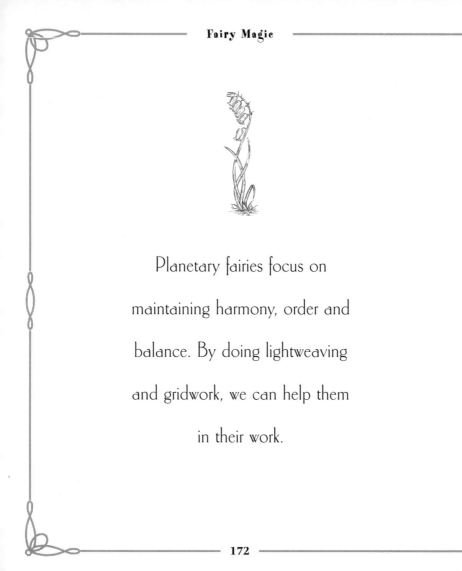

Planetary fairies focus on

maintaining harmony, order and

balance. By doing lightweaving

and gridwork, we can help them

in their work.

ADVANCED RAINBOW MEDITATION

Practise the rainbow light meditation on page 148. Add a literal twist: instead of visualizing the rainbow ribbon of light flowing straight through you from the top of the head out through the soles of the feet and the lower trunk, see it twisted gently in a soft helix. Imagine that the rainbow is made up of many tiny strands of light. The light is love. The strands spread out over your head and out into the earth as moving rivers of multi-coloured light. The lights are carried by the planetary fairies into far reaches of space, and around the earth. See the lights merge into glowing grids of energy lines that criss-cross the planet.

Turn your attention inward. Notice how the strands of light weave together in patterns in your body. Breathe the light deep into you, watching it

penetrate deeper and deeper, down through the
skin, into the tissue, into the bone, down into the
very level of the cells. The light brings healing into
the depths of your being. With every breath, you
feel fresher, lighter, better. Exhale the rainbow light.

As the breath restores you, become aware of
a change in you. You yourself are a pattern of
energy lines, along which beams of coloured
light move in incredible beauty. The lines may
be straight and grid-like, or circular, swirls or
spirals. This is your own energy pattern, unique
to you, your 'fingerprint' of light.

Repeat the affirmation three times:
I am the beauty of love and light.

Notice how responsive is your energy pattern.
It reacts to every thought, every feeling. Its

brightness increases and decreases. It expands and contracts. It has no finite boundaries, but reaches out into infinite space, connecting you to all things in the cosmos. Allow yourself to radiate peace, love and beauty. Notice the energy pattern, and how you feel. Observe in detail what you look like as the energy of love and beauty.

Repeat the affirmation three times:
I flow in total harmony with All That Is.

Notice how you feel being in harmony – emotions, physical sensations. Become aware of how the rainbow energy flows through your body.

USING THE RAINBOW MATRIX

Practise the advanced rainbow meditation until it becomes easy for you to shift your consciousness into patterns and flows of light. You will soon find

you can make this shift without having to enter
into formal meditation.

Weave your light into the energy patterns that
you see around you: things in nature, places and
other people. Weave the light with the intent of
love. You do not need to have a specific purpose.
In fact, it is better to allow the energy to be used
according to the highest purpose and need, and it
will be so directed by the planetary fairies.

Lightweaving reinforces the connectedness of
all things. Love is the force that maintains order
and harmony.

In gridwork, the strands of light are sent into the
earth. In your attuned consciousness, become
aware of patterns of energy beneath you. Every
place has its own energy signature, which can be

made clairvoyantly visible to you as patterns of auric light. In observing the lines, you may discover how certain things are connected to each other. You may see places that are energized by great vitality, and others that are in need of vitalization.

Send strands of rainbow light into the earth, and observe where they are taken. The planetary fairies will give you intuitive prompts when it is most beneficial for you to tune in to this kind of work.

Fairy magic on your own

The Golden Door is the opening to the fairy realm. When you picked up this book, you entered onto the path leading to the Golden Door. Reading the book and doing the activities and meditations have opened the door.

Now that the door is opened, you will be inspired and guided to expand your work with the fairy realm in ways unique to you and your talents, abilities and skills. The emergence of global village and global mind increases the need for human beings to understand, see and *feel* their connection to each other and all things. The state of the world is not someone else's fault, but everyone's responsibility. Fairy work helps to raise that awareness.

On a more personal level, fairy work is rewarding and life-changing. Just open the Golden Door and follow the light.

About the Author

Rosemary Ellen Guiley, Ph.D. is a best-selling author whose work is devoted to helping others achieve their goals and find fulfilment in life, creativity and work through 'visionary living'. She is president of her own company, Visionary Living, Inc. Ms Guiley presents workshops and seminars on a wide range of spiritual and self-help topics, such as working with the fairy and angelic realms, developing the intuition, understanding dreams, and deepening the spiritual path through prayer and meditation.

Her other books published by Thorsons are *Ask the Angels*, *An Angel in Your Pocket*, *A Miracle in Your Pocket* and *The Angels' Tarot*. In addition, Ms Guiley has authored other books on other subjects, including dreams, intuition, prayer, mysticism and mystical experience, saints, angels, ghosts, sacred sites, and more. Her work has been translated into 13 languages, selected by major book clubs, and cited for excellence.

Ms Guiley lives with her husband, Tom, in Arnold, Maryland, USA. Her websites are:
http://www.rosemaryguiley.com and
Visionary Living, http://www.visionaryliving.com.